SOOTHING

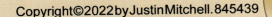

To order additional copies of this book, contact:
Xlibris
844-714-8691
www.Xlibris.com
Orders@Xlibris.com

ISBN: 978-1-6698-4166-1 (sc)
ISBN: 978-1-6698-4167-8 (hc)
ISBN: 978-1-6698-4164-7 (e)

Print information available on the last page

Rev. date: 12/27/2023

FOODIE

Acknowledgment

For my Mother and Father. Thank you for teaching me about nutrition and instructing me to live a healthy lifestyle. I honor you always and I am forever grateful. I also would like to acknowledge and give thanks to God for blessing me with this gift so that I can be a blessing to my family and friends and to everyone of my faithful readers and supporters.

The Precious Gift Of Life God Gives Is To Be Maintained
To Live A Joyful Healthy Life And Prosper And Obtain
An Abundant Healthy Lifestyle That Will Surely Help You Grow
To Be Nutritive And Fruitful Healthful Everywhere You Go

I Am Panacea
I Am Here To Help You
With Good Nourishment
That Will Bring Good Health To

1

Prosper Your Body
And Improve Your Mind
So You Will Be Productive
And Can Function Right

Be Rational And Make Sure
That You Eat 3 Meals A Day
With A Healthy Breakfast
Lunch and Dinner You Will Be Ok

3

Make Sure The Meals That You Prepare
Are Balanced When You Eat
With Vegetation
Fruits And Grain
Some Dairy
And Lean Meats

And It's Ok To Treat Yourself Too
Sometimes With A Snack
But Always Make Sure That
You Have Some Self-control With That

5

Remember Always To Make Sure You Drink Plenty Of Water With Every Meal Until You Feel You're Hydrated Regardless

H2Organic is a brand of the highest standard quality naturally pure and refreshing water custom blended with the perfect amount electrolytes and minerals to help you stay hydrated.

What You Choose To Eat And Drink
Does Affect Your Mind
When You're Wholesome In Your Thinking
You Will Be Revitalized

Your Well-being And Your Lifestyle Will Improve And You Will Find That Your Body Will Develop Very Well And You Will Thrive

9

Beneficial Vegetation Is
Very Good For You
Vegetables Are Full Of Minerals
And Good Nutrients Too

Eating Spinach And Zucchini
And Potatoes Of All Kinds
Is Important To Consider
When It's Lunch Or Dinner Time

11

Asparagus And Broccoli
Are Important To Include
Also Celery And Cauliflower
You Should Eat That Too

Eating Beet Roots
And Legumes Of A Variety
Is Good For Maturation
With A Good Sense Of Propriety

Wholesome Brothers Peanut Butter is a naturally tasty and certified organic brand of high quality peanut butter spreads that come in two kinds both Smooth Protein and Yummy Crunchy Chunky with nuts in it. Those two kinds come in a variety of different flavors that are pleasing and satisfying.

MR. PATENT AND PRICE PEANUT
"BRAND AMBASSADORS"

WHOLESOME
BROTHERS
PEANUT BUTTER

14

Including Cabbage
Kale And Mushrooms
Is Good For Your Diet

With Plenty Of Corn Cucumbers
And Abundant Supplies
Of Greens Of Every Type
And Tomatoes That Are Ripe

And Some Lettuce Should Be Added That Will Make A Lovely Salad

Fruits Are Good For You In Fact
They're Filled With Antioxidants
And Good And Healthy Vitamins
I Recommend That You Eat Them

18

Soothing Foodie Smoothie is a healthy fuel good brand of freshly made smoothies that combine nutrients, antioxidants, proteins, flavorful fruit options and plant based nourishing ingredients with more than 4,000 different made to order blend options Soothing Foodie Smoothies offers total ingredient transparency and tastes just as good as it makes you feel. Soothing Foodie Smoothie is a subsidiary of the brand Soothing Foodie

MR. PANACEA IDEA
"BRAND AMBASSADOR"

19

Eat Oranges And
All Sorts Of Berries
Pomegranates Grapes
And Cherries

Delicious Nutritious Jelly is a brand of one hundred percent natural and organic fruit spreads that are made from real fruits that come in a variety of flavors that include Peach, Raspberry, Grape, Mixed Berry, Cherry, Blueberry, Apricot, Orange, Strawberry, Apple and many more.

MR. STRAWBERRY SERGIO
"BRAND AMBASSADOR"

Lemons Limes And Grapefruits Plus Avocados And Coconuts

It's Delicious
You'll Be Well
When You Eat Every
Kind Of Melon

23

Nectarines Papayas And The Apricots Pears And Bananas

24

That's All Good
For You Eat Some
Eat Guavas Mangos
And Eat Plums

Consume Dairy
In Your Routine
When Eating
It's Full Of Protein

26

Sunny's Milk and Honey is a high quality healthy brand of milk and honey. Our pure organic dairy milk is a source of calcium and has more of the proteins and nutrients that your body needs for everything from brain development, to building lean muscle and strong healthy bones. Our milk provides nourishment and vitality to the world and comes in a variety of different kinds that include real cows milk, oat milk, almond milk, coconut milk, soy milk and much more. Our milk has a rich and creamy taste and comes in quarts, 1/2 gallons and gallons to fulfill your needs as you grow and prosper.

SUNNY SUNSHINE
"BRAND AMBASSADOR"

And Calcium
And Probiotics
When You Eat
Add Dairy Products

Milk And Cheese Of Every Kind
Is Good For You Yes I Advise
You To Include That And Combine
Some Butter To Your Meals Sometimes

29

At Times Have Dessert Between Lunch And Dinner Time Cuisine

30

With Some Yogurt
Or Ice Cream
That Is Good
For You Indeed

31

Eating Grain Is Also Great
With Fiber And Carbohydrates
There Full Of Antioxidants
Grain Is Important To Digest

Sunny's Milk and honey is a high quality healthy brand of milk and honey. Our top quality honey is made naturally by bees from the nectar they gather straight from the hive. Our honey does not expire and does not contain any additives or preservatives. Our signature honey is thicker and richer and we offer the best tasting clean varietal blends to ensure it's consistency. Our honey comes in premium pure or unfiltered raw and comes directly from the source.

SUNNY SUNSHINE
"BRAND AMBASSADOR"

33

Have Some Oats
And Barley Too
For Breakfast
Or Eat Cereal

34

Foodie O's is a yummy brand of cereal made with organic ingredients that combine whole grains for a balance of nutrition and taste. Our gluten - free cereal made with whole grain oats, whole grain corn, whole grain rice and grains are home grown, milled and toasted resulting in a delicious and unique cereal. This is a cholesterol free cereal with fiber, vitamins, minerals and honey kissed goodness.

35

Eat Plenty Rice
Of Every Kind
Eat Quinoa Millet
Corn Or Rye

Make Sure You Have Plenty Bread That Is What I Recommend

37

Chosen Dough Bread Co is a wholesome and organic manufacturer and distributer of a multitude of healthy breads that include white, whole wheat, rye, pretzels multigrain, baguette, ciabatta, challah, brioche, flat, bagels, pita pancakes, focaccia, corn bread, Hawaiian rolls, raisin bread, matzo, bread sticks, crepes, croissants and much more.

THE SWEET TANNED WHEAT MAN
"BRAND AMBASSADOR"

38

And Every Sort
Of Pasta Too
And Chia Yes
That's Good For You

Eating Meat Is
What You Need
To Ingest
Nutritious Protein

Elite Meats is a good healthy brand of all kinds of different meats. We offer the highest quality choices of farm raised organic meats of a wide variety that includes chicken, beef, turkey, seafood and much more. We deliver the best cuts of meat without artificial flavors or fillers, and without MSG because in our meat quality is the most important ingredient

MR. & MRS. THEW GREW
"BRAND AMBASSADORS"

Plus Vitamins
Do Help Your System
To Increase
Metabolism

Fruitful & Truly Nutritive Chewy Vitamins is a high quality brand of nutritional supplement multivitamins that will support your wellness needs for brain health, bone and joint health, digestive health, energy support, eye health, hair skin and nail health, heart health, immunity support, stress and mood support and sleep support. Our vitamins come in a wide variety for different ages, genders and health goals. Our vitamins provide the quality, purity and potency you need that will make you stronger and protect you longer.

MR. & MRS. GROOVY EBULLIENCE BEAR
"BRAND AMBASSADORS"

43

In Meats There Are
Omega 3's
That Oils Good
And Is Healthy

Victual Oil is a healthy and nourishing brand of cooking oil made of a natural blend of gluten free plant based oils and oil seeds. This oil is helpful in preventing food from sticking to cookware such as skillets and baking pans and utensils such as spatulas, wooden spoons, measuring cups and skewers. Our oil comes in a variety of different kinds that include olive oil, avocado oil, coconut oil, peanut oil, sunflower oil, sesame oil, red palm oil, grape seed oil, vegetable oil and many more that will adapt to your cooking style.

45

Eat Chicken
And All Types Of Fishes
When Preparing
Healthy Dishes

Include Turkey
In Your Meals
Or Healthy Tri-Tip
Is Ideal

47

Also Meatloaf Is Ok Or Sausage And Eggs I Must Say

48

Is Great To Eat
Or Try Ground Beef
Or Add Crustaceans
To Your Feast

FRESH GROUND BEEF

49

When You're Eating Make Sure That You Understand Proportions Don't Eat More Or Less Than Your Own Body Supports

50

Check Yourself Regularly
Make Sure That Your Weight
Is In Proportion To Your Height
And Your Body's Feeling Great

Make Sure Your 3 Meals Are Equidistant Times Apart From Your Dinner To Your Lunch

To Your Breakfast When You Start

52

I Am Panacea
And All Of This Is True
When You Do This You'll Be Enriched
Nourished And Healthy Too

Give Thanks To God
Every Time You Eat
Saying Prayer Is Reverent
And More Importantly

54

Be Very Grateful
For Your Food
Some People Do
Have Less Than You

Interior Floor Plan Diagram

19,100 SQFT

BIG WINDOW

DRIVE THROUGH WINDOW #1

DRIVE THROUGH WINDOW #2

DRIVE THROUGH SERVICE WORKER AREA

191 FT LONG

15 FT

4 FT

30 FT WIDE X 38 FT LONG

18 FT WIDE X 129 FT LONG

100 FT WIDE

#8 PANACEAS PALACE

3 FT

9 FT WIDE X 9 FT LONG

#6

GREETERS

#4 FOODIES FORUM STAGE

ONR 1,056 SQFT
24 FT WIDE X 44 FT LONG
#1 INTERNATIONAL ISLANDS

#7

#7

ROOFING

SERVICE WINDOW

#5 THE CONVALESCENCE KITCHEN

52 FT WIDE

18 FT LONG

6 FT

BACK DOOR

#6

3 FT

18 FT

6 FT

38 FT

4 FT

#7

TABLES AND CHAIRS

ENTRANCE #2

6 FT

ANTECHAMBER AREA

9 FT WIDE X 18 FT LONG

#2 SOOTHING FOODIE SMOOTHIES

#7

#7

#7

30 FT WIDE X 47 FT LONG

9 FT WIDE X 18 FT LONG

#3 GARDEN OF FEED'N

4 FT

#6

3 FT

7 FT

47 FT

COUCHES AND SITTING AREAS

9 FT WIDE X 18 FT LONG

#6

3 FT

BIG WINDOW

38 FT

6 FT

ENTRANCE #1

38 FT

53 FT

53 FT

Correlative Description

#1 INTERNATIONAL ISLANDS – A SELF-SERVICE CAFETERIA STRUCTURE THAT FEATURES 7 CONTINENTS AND 195 COUNTRIES WITH SERVERS FROM THOSE COUNTRIES ASIA 48, AFRICA 54, N. AMERICA 23, S. AMERICA 12, EUROPE 44, AUSTRALIA/OCEANIA 14, ANTARTICA

#2 SOOTHING FOODIE SMOOTHIES - SMOOTHIE AND JUICE BAR WITH MORE THAN 4,000 DIFFERENT DRINK OPTIONS

#3 GARDEN OF FEED'N – FARMERS MARKET /STORE OF FRESH PRODUCE

#4 STAGE (FOODIES FORUM) – FOR EVENTS AND PERFORMANCES /PUPPET SHOWS AND A PLACE WHERE PANACEA AND THE CONVALESCENCE WILL PERFORM AND ALSO A PLACE WHERE OTHER RECORDED PUBLIC SPEAKING EVENTS WILL TAKE PLACE

#5 THE CONVALESCENCE KITCHEN - SPECIAL ORDERS PREPARED RIGHT IN FRONT OF CUSTOMERS AND SERVED TO THEM

#6 BATHROOMS

#7 GLOBAL SOCIAL - DINING AND EATING AREA WITH MUCH SEATING

#8 PANACEA'S PALACE / PLAY AREA - A LARGE PLAY STRUCTURE FOR KIDS AND CHILDCARE WHERE THEY CAN EXPLORE AND ALSO LEARN ABOUT EATING HEALTHY

Now That You Know
What Foods Are Healthy
You Can Make
Good Meals Yourself See

Restaurant Dimensions

19,100 Sq ft

100ft Wide & 191 ft Long

Foodie funding is the monetary system in the "Soothing Foodie" Restaurants. We have "Cash Cuisine Coins" called REPASTS, they are made of solid gold. With this regimen one REPAST = $35 U.S. Dollars. This gold is applicable and can be utilized at Soothing Foodie and exchanged for any food orders at the International Islands, the Convalescence Kitchen, for Soothing Foodie Smoothies, in the Garden of Feed'n to order products and fresh produce, to place orders in the Global Social area, at Foodie's Forum during events and in Panacea's Palace. Here we call it Foodie Funds.

With Some Diligence
And Effort
You'll Have Some
New Cuisine Methods

The workers are called CUTIES and they are here to serve
the accommodations comfort and healthy meals you deserve

Exterior Perigon Diagram 360 Degrees

FRONT ENTRANCE

Signage 1

RIGHT SIDE VIEW

THIS IS AN ORIGINAL ARCHITECTURAL DEPICTION OF THE "SOOTHING FOODIE" RESTAURANT CREATED BY JUSTIN JEROME MITCHELL "THE SUPREME JUSTICE OF SUSTENANCE" & THE WORLD'S RICHEST RESTAURATEUR IN HIS THIRD OFFICIAL BOOK PUBLICATION TITLED "SOOTHING FOODIE." THIS IS A THREE HUNDRED AND SIXTY DEGREE PERSPECTIVE VIEW FROM ALL FOUR SIDES OF THE BUILDING. ALL SIGNAGE IS ALSO INCLUDED IN THIS DEPICTION.

BACK VIEW

Signage 2

LEFT SIDE VIEW

Do The Very Best You Can To Make Good Healthy Eating Plans

JOURNAL

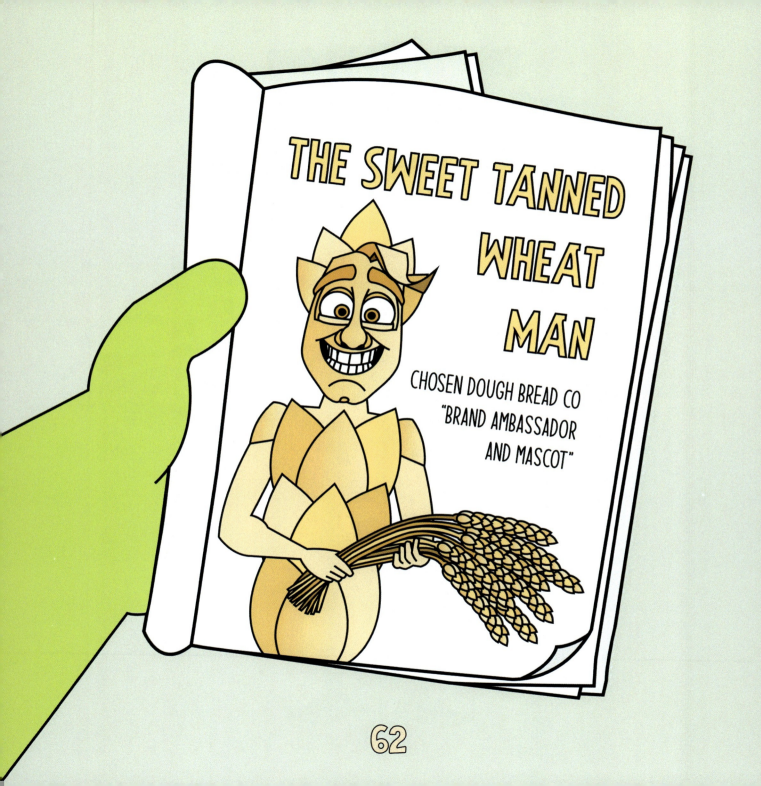

Eat Foods From Cultures Of Every Kind And Always Have An Open Mind

parfait

taco

lumpia

sushi

pizza

Each Way Of Life Differs However Food Can Bring Them All Together

chow mein

sabji

jibarito

tortilla espanola

With Plenty Options
On Your Plate
There's Many Ways
You Can Relate

To Friends And Family
And Create
Good Food
As You Communicate

The Soothing Foodie SCOOTIE is used to deliver orders
From our restaurant sent to you fresh from the store

Single Seat

Scootie Logo

SCOOTIE

5 ft High

Front View

Side View

14 ft Long

For transporting food orders

Cooling Side

Heating Side

SCOOTIE

Back View

7 ft Wide

Healthy Eating's Easy When You Read Every Ingredient

Friends,
you will love this perfect combination of healthy and refreshing flavors these granola balls are filled with nutrients that are all great for your health.

Nutrition Facts
10 balls per bag.

vitamin d	0%
vitamin c	0%
calcium	0%
iron	0%
potassium	0%
Calories	**200**
total fat	0%

Ingredients

- amazing raisins
- very berry cherries
- strong almonds
- sunflower power seeds
- honey yummy oats

VIABLE
RELIABALLS
GRANOLA
trail mix

67

Viable Reliaballs is a brand of clean simple and wholesome handmade balls of granola that are made of organic ingredients super-food oats and ancient grains that have holistic healing properties to support digestive health. Our granola balls are both healthy and tasty and will give you long lasting energy.

VIABLE RELIABALLS

GRANOLA

trail mix

Restaurants Are Ok Sometimes But It's Better To Have Supplies

Warehouse Dimensions

40,320 Sq ft

140ft Wide & 288ft Long

48 ft High

48 ft High

14ft High

SOOTHINGFOODIE

HEALTHIER   NUTRITION

SOOTHINGFOODIE
WAREHOUSE

69

Learn To Cook
For Yourself When
You Eat Your Victuals
Or Meal Prep

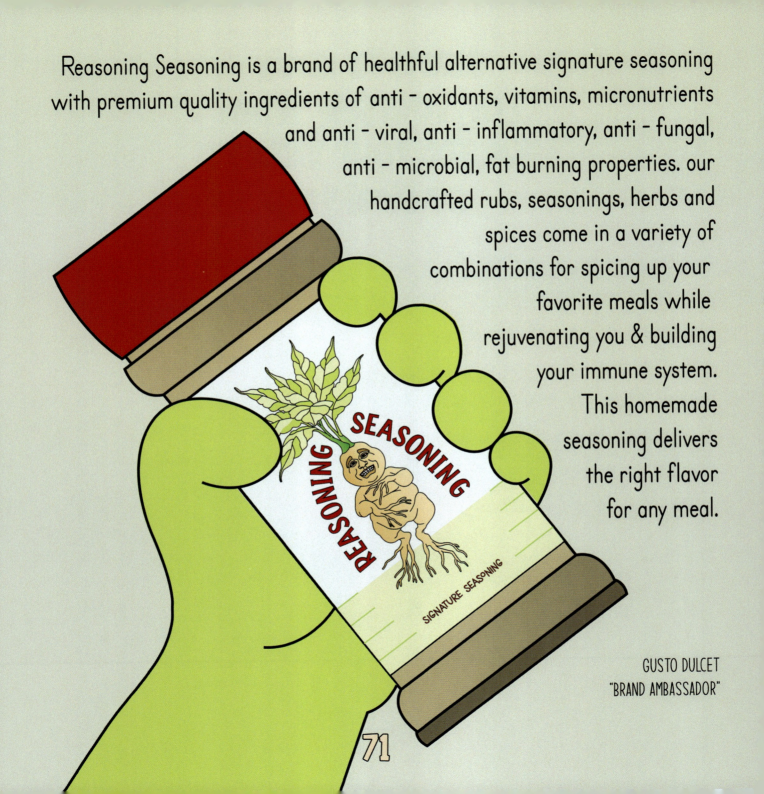

Reasoning Seasoning is a brand of healthful alternative signature seasoning with premium quality ingredients of anti‑oxidants, vitamins, micronutrients and anti‑viral, anti‑inflammatory, anti‑fungal, anti‑microbial, fat burning properties. our handcrafted rubs, seasonings, herbs and spices come in a variety of combinations for spicing up your favorite meals while rejuvenating you & building your immune system. This homemade seasoning delivers the right flavor for any meal.

GUSTO DULCET
"BRAND AMBASSADOR"

71

Yes Eat At Home
And Prepare Meals
Ahead Of Time
And Keep Them Sealed

Sometimes So If You're On The Go You'll Have Some Sustenance You Know

The name of this Food Truck is "BEAUTY"

14 ft High

SOOTHING FOODIE

VIABLE RELIABILLS GRANOLA

The Soothing Foodie Food Trucks are sent out to many places In all communities so everyone can have a taste

8 ft Wide

18 ft Long

Then You Can Eat
At Your Own Pace
And Really Enjoy
How It Tastes

Journal The Food
You Intake
Then You Will
Make Less Mistakes

75

Know What You Ate And Avoided And Be Aware Of All Your Choices

Create Weekly
Menus Too
For All Meal Times
Of Your Food

You'll Be Prepared To Review That So You Will Know What To Do

Also Make A Grocery List Every Week And Stick To It

Keep Track Of All You Require And Don't Run Out Of Supplies

All Your Eating Habits Should Lead You To Have Success keep It Simple Make Sure All You Consume Is Always Fresh

Everyday Be Active
For At Least 30 Minutes
Surround Yourself With Those
In Support Of Your Way Of Living

82

I Am Panacea Do All This
And Be Consistent
You'll Be Happy Sanitary
Vivacious And More Efficient

Make Use
Of Relaxation
Meditate You'll
Be Alright

84

And Make Sure
You Are Resting
For 8 Hours
Every Night

Gain Nutrition Knowledge
Your Relationship With Food
Effects Your Health And Future
Learn These Skills And You'll Improve

86

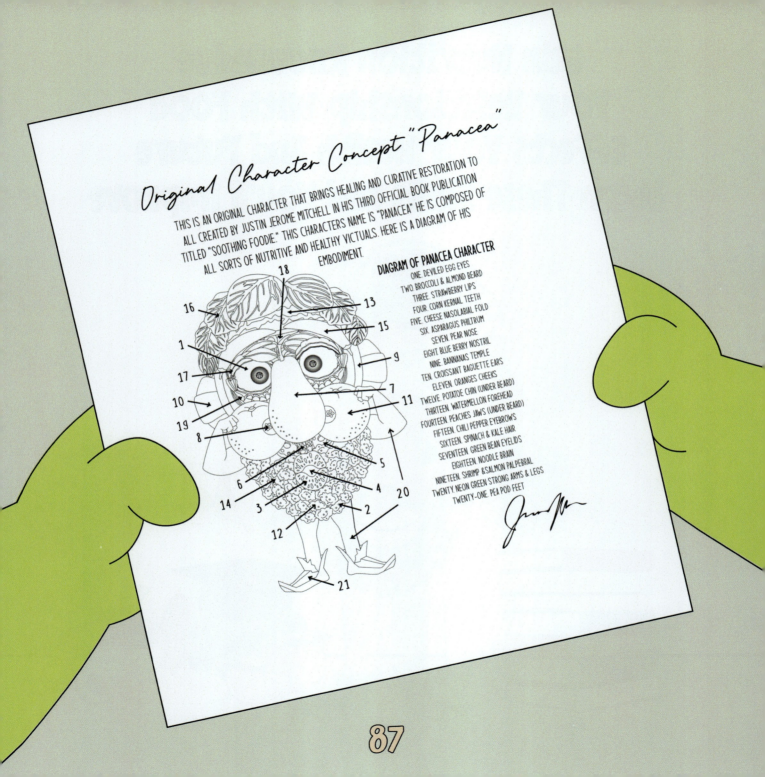

Original Character Concept "Panacea"

THIS IS AN ORIGINAL CHARACTER THAT BRINGS HEALING AND CURATIVE RESTORATION TO ALL CREATED BY JUSTIN JEROME MITCHELL IN HIS THIRD OFFICIAL BOOK PUBLICATION TITLED "SOOTHING FOODIE." THIS CHARACTERS NAME IS "PANACEA" HE IS COMPOSED OF ALL SORTS OF NUTRITIVE AND HEALTHY VICTUALS. HERE IS A DIAGRAM OF HIS EMBODIMENT.

DIAGRAM OF PANACEA CHARACTER

ONE. DEVILED EGG EYES
TWO. BROCCOLI & ALMOND BEARD
THREE. STRAWBERRY LIPS
FOUR. CORN KERNAL TEETH
FIVE. CHEESE NASOLABIAL FOLD
SIX. ASPARAGUS PHILTRUM
SEVEN. PEAR NOSE
EIGHT. BLUE BERRY NOSTRIL
NINE. BANNANAS TEMPLE
TEN. CROISSANT BAGUETTE EARS
ELEVEN. ORANGES CHEEKS
TWELVE. POTATOE CHIN (UNDER BEARD)
THIRTEEN. WATERMELLON FOREHEAD
FOURTEEN. PEACHES JAWS (UNDER BEARD)
FIFTEEN. CHILI PEPPER EYEBROWS
SIXTEEN. SPINACH & KALE HAIR
SEVENTEEN. GREEN BEAN EYELIDS
EIGHTEEN. NOODLE BRAIN
NINETEEN. SHRIMP &SALMON PALPEBRAL
TWENTY. NEON GREEN STRONG ARMS & LEGS
TWENTY-ONE. PEA POD FEET

Respect Your Body
Appreciate The Life
That God
Has Given

Practice Mindfulness
Of Everything
That You
Put In It

89

Attainable Objectives
When Nutrition Is Selected
Is Good For Your Aptitude
And The Health Of
Your Brains Perception

Reward Yourself As You Improve
And Go Do What You Like
As You Develop Health
And Strength Then
You Will Be Alright

Having Self-Discipline Is Not As Hard As It Seems

Healthy Habits
And Routines
Will Build Up
Your Self-Esteem

Reflect On
All Your Habits
When Their Good
Or If Their Bad

Be Conscious Of Unhealthy Eating Cravings That You've Had

Review Your Journal
That You Use
To Describe
What You Ate

If The Reason For Your Eating Is Not Hunger Then Create A List Of How Your Feeling When You Eat That Indicates

Your Frame Of Mind
And If It Isn't Healthy Then Replace
Those Habits With More Helpful
Healthy Ones For
Goodness Sakes

I Am Panacea
When You Do This You Will Truly
Be Fulfilled With Provision
Because This Is
Soothing Foodie

100

Printed in the United States
by Baker & Taylor Publisher Services